# Colors of
# RUSSIA

by Shannon Zemlicka
illustrations by Jeni Reeves

COLORS OF THE WORLD

Carolrhoda Books, Inc. / Minneapolis

*For my mother, Brenda Barefield—the first person who encouraged me to write—S.Z.*

*Thanks to Rachel May of the Department of Russian Studies at Macalester College, Dina Drits, and Vladimir Drits for their assistance with the Russian translations—S.Z.*

*The illustrator wishes to thank Nancy Kraft, R.D., L.D., whose photographs and insights about Russia proved very illuminating.—J.R.*

*This book is available in two editions:*
Library binding by Carolrhoda Books, Inc., a division of Lerner Publishing Group
Soft cover by First Avenue Editions, an imprint of Lerner Publishing Group
241 First Avenue North
Minneapolis, MN 55401 U.S.A.

Website address: www.lernerbooks.com

Library of Congress Cataloging-in-Publication Data

Zemlicka, Shannon.
   Colors of Russia / by Shannon Zemlicka.
     p.  cm. — (Colors of the world)
   Includes index.
   ISBN 1-57505-513-9 (lib. bdg. : alk. paper)
   ISBN 1-57505-564-3 (pbk. : alk. paper)
   1. Russia (Federation)—Juvenile literature. I. Title. II. Series.
DK510.23.Z46 2002
947—dc21                          00-010306

Manufactured in the United States of America
1 2 3 4 5 6 – JR – 07 06 05 04 03 02

ARCTIC OCEAN

SIBERIA

ASIAN RUSSIA

EUROPEAN
RUSSIA

R U S S I A

Saint Petersburg

Lake Baikal

Moscow

URAL MOUNTAINS

Caspian Sea

PACIFIC
OCEAN

R U S S I A

EUROPE

ASIA

AFRICA

AUSTRALIA

# Introduction

Russia is the largest country in the world. It is almost twice as big as the United States. Russia stretches across two continents, Europe and Asia. European Russia is west of the Ural Mountains. The nation's capital, Moscow, is located here. Asian Russia is east of the mountains.

Along with mountains, you can find many kinds of land in Russia. The tundra is a cold, flat area in the north. Forests and flat, grassy plains called steppes (STEPS) lie south of the tundra.

For hundreds of years, rich, powerful rulers called czars (ZAHRZ) and czarinas (zahr-EE-nuhz) ran Russia. Then these rulers lost power. For most of the 1900s, Russia and many of its neighbors were part of a larger country called the Soviet Union. In 1991, the Soviet Union split into fifteen different countries. Russia was one of them. About 146 million people live in Russia. They speak many different languages, but the official language is Russian.

# Yellow

**Жёлтый Цвет**—*zheltyi tsvet*

**(ZHOHL-tyeh TSVYEHT)**

A beautiful **yellow** palace stands near Saint Petersburg. The Alexander Palace was once the home of a girl named Anastasia (ahn-uh-STAH-see-yuh). She was the daughter of a Russian czar, Nicholas II. Anastasia spent much of her time with her three older sisters and younger brother. The girls often wore matching dresses. They bicycled past sparkling fountains, played with dozens of dolls, and yawned through boring English lessons. They picked flowers and painted pictures of them. Anastasia, the clown of the group, could make almost anyone smile.

The czars and their families lived lives of ease and wealth. But under their rule, almost everyone else lived hard lives. People worked long hours but were still very poor. Finally, in 1917, a group of Russians forced Czar Nicholas to give up his power. The next year, Czar Nicholas and his entire family were killed. But for many years, some people believed that Anastasia had not died. Her story has been remembered in books and movies.

6

# Red

*Красный Цвет—kransyi isvet*

**(KRAHS-nyeh TSVYEHT)**

After Czar Nicholas lost power, Russia's government changed. The Communist Party and its **Red** Army began to lead the country. This army was named for the color of the Communist flag. On November 7 each year, people carried red flags and balloons through Moscow's Red Square to celebrate the anniversary of the Communist government.

At first, the Communist government seemed like a good idea, but it did not work well. The new government owned all the land, homes, and businesses. It planned to share everything with the people. Then, no one would be poor anymore. But no matter how hard people worked, they earned little money. They were not allowed to vote for a new government. Anyone who complained might be put in prison or killed.

The Communist government lost power in 1991. The Russian people could then own homes and businesses and vote for the leaders they choose. Many people still have trouble earning enough money to live. But the Russians have survived many hardships over their long history. They have not lost hope for a better future.

# Blue

## *Синий Цвет—sinii tsvet*

## (SEE-nyeh TSVYEHT)

Would you like to add one year to your life? Here's an idea from a Russian legend. Just dip your hands in the cold, **blue** water of Lake Baikal (bye-KAHL). Would you rather have five extra years? Dunk your feet in the lake. And if you're brave enough to go for a swim? The legend promises you twenty-five years—unless the cold kills you on the spot!

Water can't really add years to a person's life. But Lake Baikal is still a special place. More than five thousand feet deep, it is the deepest lake in the world. Its water is clean enough to drink. Fish and seals provide food for the people who live near the lake. These Russians enjoy living near the icy water. They call Lake Baikal the "sacred sea." To them, it is the most beautiful place in the world.

# White

## *Белый Цвет—belyi tsvet*
## (BYEH-lyeh TSVYEHT)

The Chukchi (CHOOK-chee) people live on the **white,** snow-covered land of northeastern Siberia, a huge region in Asian Russia. For hundreds of years, many Chukchis based their way of life on the area's reindeer. Each family taught its children how to care for the reindeer. The Chukchis used reindeer fur to make clothing and shelter.

Then, during the mid-1900s, the Communist government took over the reindeer herds. It made many Chukchis settle and work in towns. The government sent Chukchi children to live at boarding schools far from home. There the children learned to speak Russian. Years later, when they returned home, some had forgotten the Chukchi language. And they had not learned how to care for the reindeer.

Some Chukchis want to return to their former customs. They have asked the Russian government to give the reindeer back. They are teaching their children the Chukchi language and traditions. They hope they can regain a lost way of life.

# Green

## Зелёный Цвет—*zelenyi tsvet*
## (zehl-YOH-nyeh TSVYEHT)

In the summer, tall **green** grass covers many parts of southern Russia. This flat land is called the steppe. Not much rain falls on the steppe. But the soil is very good for crops. Farmers grow wheat, oats, barley, and rye. These grains provide food for people and animals.

About three thousand years ago, the steppe was the home of the Scythians (SITH-ee-uhnz). They were nomads, people who move from one place to another. The Scythians used the horses for milk, meat, and transportation. When a herd of horses had eaten all the grass in one area, the animals moved to a new spot. As the horses moved, the Scythians packed their felt tents and followed them. These nomads became known throughout Europe and Asia for their ability to tame and ride horses.

14

# Brown

## *Коричневый Цвет—korichnevyi tsvet*
## (koh-REECH-nee-vyeh TSVYEHT)

Snow falls.  Icy winds sting your face.  It is winter in Russia—time to wear an *ushanka* (oo-SHAHN-kuh), a furry **brown** hat.  Many Russians wear fur to stay warm through the long, cold winter.   Ushankas are especially warm because they have flaps that fold down over your ears.

In Russia, winter lasts for many months.  Most of the country is covered with snow for half the year or more.  In the far north, the ground stays frozen all year long.  Almost nothing grows there.  But Russia's long winter has its good side, too.  People make the most of the weather by sledding, skiing, ice skating, and playing hockey.

# Gold

## *Золотой Цвет—zolotoi tsvet*

## (zoh-lah-TOY TSVYEHT)

When you see a Russian building with shiny **gold** domes on top of it, you are probably looking at a Russian Orthodox church. The domes are called onion domes because they are shaped like onions. Russians say this unusual design keeps snow from piling up on the domes. Many domes are more than five hundred years old and are covered with real gold.

Inside the church, you might find many other gold objects. Beautiful paintings called icons (EYE-kahnz) hang on the walls. Icons are often painted with gold or copper. Orthodox priests sometimes wear gold robes and hats. Gold candlesticks and lamps provide light. Many churches have gold statues, too. Why is there so much golden beauty? For the people who built the breathtaking churches of Russia, using gold was a way of honoring God.

# Black

## Цёрный Цвет—*chernyi tsvet*
## (CHOR-nyeh TSVYEHT)

Have you ever eaten a food made of tiny **black** balls even smaller than your little fingernail?  If so, you have probably eaten caviar (KA-vee-ahr), or salted fish eggs.  Russian caviar is one of the most expensive foods in the world.  Most people do not eat it often.  But for a special meal, Russians might eat caviar with sour cream and pancakes, called *bliny* (blee-NEE).

Most Russian caviar comes from sturgeon (STUR-juhn) in the Caspian Sea.  These fish can weigh as much as 2,500 pounds.  They can live to be 150 years old.  But almost no sturgeon survives that long.  To get eggs for making caviar, fishers must catch and kill female sturgeon.  Russia has laws that limit fishing to certain times of the year.  But many people break the laws.  Unless fishers stop killing so many sturgeon, caviar may become a food of the past.

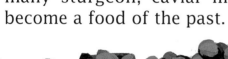

19

# Orange

**Оранжевый Цвет**—*oranzhevyi tsvet*

**(oh-RAHN-zee-vyeh TSVYEHT)**

In the forests of southeastern Russia lives an amazing **orange** animal—the Siberian tiger. It is the biggest cat in the world. Siberian tigers can leap the length of a pickup truck, with room to spare. They can jump over a fence as high as a tall person. But these strong, beautiful cats may not wander Russia's forests much longer. Only a few hundred live in the wild. Another five hundred live in zoos.

What is causing trouble for Siberian tigers? People hunt them as a way to make money. And loggers have been cutting down many trees to sell the wood. As the forests get smaller, tigers have fewer places to live. The animals that tigers eat also lose their homes.

To save the tigers, the Russian government has set aside land where hunting and logging are not allowed. Rangers patrol the land to keep hunters away. So far, these steps seem to be helping. Scientists think that fewer tigers are dying. That's good news for the tigers and the many people who love them.

# Gray

### Серый Цвет—*seryi tsvet*
### (SAYR-yeh TSVYEHT)

Gray marble archways stretch as far you can see. Fancy lamps hang from the ceiling. Colorful stained-glass panels dazzle your eyes. Are you in a museum or a castle? No—you are in a subway station in Moscow! A subway is a train that runs in underground tunnels. The Moscow subway is called the Metro. More than seven million people use it every day. For about thirty-five cents, you can ride as long and as far as you like.

The first part of the Metro was built in the 1930s. The country's leaders wanted it to be the finest subway in the world. People used to joke about how nice the Metro would be. They said that mothers would have to make their children wash their hands before riding, so they wouldn't get the trains dirty! The Moscow Metro is not quite that fancy. But everyone who sees it agrees that it is one of the most beautiful subways in the world.

23

# Index